Feasts of the Bible
Participant Guide

Sam Nadler

Developed with Natalia Fomin

This Participant Guide accompanies the

Feasts of the Bible 6-Session DVD-Based Study
(ISBN 9781596364646 or 9781596364653)

with

Feasts of the Bible Leader Guide
(ISBN 9781596364660)

Feasts of the Bible Participant Guide
© 2011 Bristol Works, Inc.
Rose Publishing, LLC
P.O. Box 3473
Peabody, Massachusetts 01961-3473 USA
www.hendricksonrose.com

Image Credits: Cover and p. 31 Silver Plate for Passover ©diligent; Cover Shofar ©Mordechai Meiri; p. 7 Ancient Prayer Book ©Nir Levy; p. 23 Wine and Matzoh ©Roman Sigaev; p. 30 Matzo on the Holiday ©gilya; p. 39 Loaves of Bread ©Maria Toutoudaki; p. 53 Angel Blowing a Horn ©Mark Strozier; p. 57 Challah ©Vadim Kozlovsky; p. 58 Shofar ©Howard Sandler; p. 67, 71 Ark of the Covenant ©James Steidl; p. 71 Ibex in the Negev ©Tal Naveh; p. 73 Prayers at the Western Wall © Dejan Gileski; p. 81 Lulav and Etrog ©Carly Rose Hennigan; p. 85 Prayer of Jew in Western Wall in Jerusalem on Sukkot ©Mikhail Levit; p. 86 Sukkot (Sukkah) ©Tova Teitelbaum.

Printed in the United States of America
June 2019, 18th printing

Contents

About This Study

Many times history may look like a series of events occurring randomly and haphazardly, but we know that history is "His Story"—it's God's story of restoring us to himself. In order to understand the present, we have to look back and appreciate how we got here and what it took to bring us to where we are now. Looking back can give us confidence to press on toward the future God has prepared for us in Messiah. The seven appointed feasts in the Bible reveal how God's redemptive program is woven throughout history with the redemptive thread of Messiah's sacrifice for us.

In this study, Dr. Sam Nadler will take you on a pilgrimage through the seven feasts of Israel. This study begins at the place where the need for redemption was born, in the Garden of Eden, when sin entered the world and our Sabbath rest was broken. Then you will journey through the path of redemption pictured in the biblical feasts. These six sessions will help you arrive at a greater understanding of God's unfailing love for us all and a deeper appreciation of his provision of the perfect Lamb prepared before the foundations of the world.

About the Author

Sam Nadler is a Jewish believer in Jesus who has a passion to communicate the Good News to his people, and to see discipleship established in Jewish communities around the world.

Serving with Jews for Jesus, Sam established the Jews for Jesus New York City branch in 1975. Later as the President of Chosen People Ministries, he helped build international outreach, congregational planting and leadership development in Israel, the Ukraine, Germany, South America, Canada as well as the United States.

Today as president of Word of Messiah Ministries, Sam is continuing to develop leaders and outreach to make a worldwide impact for the gospel to Jew and Gentile alike. Sam also reaches out to the Christian community teaching them to better understand the Jewish roots of their faith so they'll be able to more effectively reach out with the Good News of Messiah, as well as more fully appreciate believers' unique unity in Messiah and the ongoing testimony of God's faithfulness to his promises.

Sam received an honorary doctoral degree from Southern Evangelical Seminary. He has authored several books including *Messiah in the Feasts of Israel, The Messianic Answer Book, Messianic Foundations,* and devotional commentaries on Jonah and Ruth.

Natalia Fomin moved from the Ukraine to the USA when she was sixteen, and a few months later she gave her life to God. Ever since, she has been in active ministry teaching the Scriptures and mentoring women. In 2004, she graduated from Moody Bible Institute with a major in Christian Ministry, along with receiving theological training. Natalia and her husband Peter reside in Charlotte, NC and are blessed with three children, Mark, Daniel and Emily.

To learn more about Word of Messiah Ministries, please visit www.wordofmessiah.org.

About the Complete DVD-Based Kit

The Kit (ISBN 9781596364646) includes everything you need to teach *Feasts of the Bible* using professionally produced video sessions, leader and participant guides, and a PowerPoint® presentation.

The Kit includes:

- DVD with 6 teaching sessions

- One printed Feasts of the Bible Participant Guide
  (ISBN 9781596364677)

- One printed Feasts of the Bible Leader Guide (ISBN 9781596364660) +
  PDF Leader Guide

- One printed *Messiah in the Feasts of Israel* handbook
  (ISBN 9780970261977)

- One *Feasts of the Bible* pamphlet which includes nine Jewish feasts and
  holidays (ISBN 9781890947583)

- *Feasts of the Bible* PowerPoint® presentation on CD-ROM
  (ISBN 9781596361775)

- PDF files for posters, fliers, handouts, and bulletin inserts for promotion.

Available at www.hendricksonrose.com,
or by calling Rose Publishing at 1-800-358-3111.
Also available wherever good Christian books are sold.

Sabbath Rest

The Theme of God's Redemptive Program

HINT

Be sure to see the key terms and charts starting on page 12.

Follow Along and Take Notes

Session 1 Outline: *Sabbath Rest*

I.   Sabbath Rest: The Theme of God's Redemptive Program

    A.   Creation

        a)   Matthew 11:28

        1.   Created in his image to:

        a)   Represent

        b)   Genesis 3:15

        c)   Restore

        d)   Exodus 20

        e)   Relate

B. Redemption

    1. Deuteronomy 5:15

    2. Restored relationship

C. Sabbath Peace

    1. Rest

    2. Sanctify (set apart)

        a) Exodus 31:13

    3. Eternity

        a) Exodus 31:17

        b) Psalm 95:11; Hebrews 4:3

        c) Sign pointing to eternal rest

4. Lord of the Sabbath

    a) Matthew 12:8

    b) John 15:5

    c) Sabbath = Promise completed in Messiah

II. Seven Feasts of Israel (Leviticus 23)

  A. Moedim = "appointments"

  B. Passover

  C. Feast of Unleavened Bread

  D. Firstfruits (Reishit)

  E. Pentecost

    1. Leviticus 23:22; Harvest

F. Feast of Trumpets (Yom HaTeruah; Rosh HaShanah)

    1. Isa. 27:13; 1 Cor. 15:51–52; 1 Thess. 4:16–18

G. Day of Atonement (Yom Kippur)

    1. Zechariah 12:10

    2. Isaiah 53:6

    3. Romans 11:23–26

H. Feast of Tabernacles (Sukkot)

    1. Zechariah 14:9

    2. Revelation 7:9, 15

Key Terms

Atonement – The covering of sin; the reconciliation between God and humanity. The final atonement was made by Jesus on behalf of sinners to bring peace between humankind and God through Jesus' death on the cross. He became our sin offering. The concept of atonement spans both Testaments, everywhere pointing to the death, burial, and resurrection of Jesus for the sins of the world.

The Exodus – The story of how God delivered the Israelites from bondage in ancient Egypt by Moses. This account is recorded in the book of Exodus.

Image of God – The spiritual character of God as described in Ephesians 4:24: "Put on the new self, which in the likeness of God has been created in righteousness and holiness of the truth."

Messiah – Hebrew *Mashiach*, literally, "anointed one" as a prince or king of Israel. The Greek equivalent of this word is *christos*, which is transliterated into English as "Christ."

Moedim – Literally "appointments" in Hebrew from Leviticus 23:2. These appointments were the scheduled times to appear before the Lord for worship and sacrifices. The feasts of Israel from Leviticus 23 were God's appointed times.

Redemptive Program – The word *redemption* means "to buy back." The Fall of Man in the Garden of Eden through sin caused separation with God and spiritual death. Since then God launched his program to restore humanity to himself. The feasts of Israel picture how God's redemptive work will be accomplished.

Sanctification – A biblical term that encompasses two aspects: Sanctification is a one-time act that sets a person apart to God at salvation, thus believers are called "saints" in the Bible; and it is also the process of spiritually maturing into the likeness of Jesus.

Sabbath – An Anglicized word for *Shabbat* that literally means "cessation" in Hebrew and is understood as "rest." In the Old Testament, the Sabbath is the seventh day of the week. Shabbat begins at sundown on Friday until sundown on Saturday and is a day of rest unto God.

Sheva – Hebrew word for the number seven. It means "completion," as seven days make a complete week. It also means "oath" or "vow." For example, the name Elizabeth in Hebrew, *Eli-sheva*, means "the oath of God."

Shabbat Shalom – The traditional Sabbath greeting in Hebrew said in Jewish communities on Shabbat, meaning "Sabbath Peace."

Ten Commandments – Part of the Law written by God on two tablets received by Moses on Mt. Sinai. These two tablets were placed in the Ark of the Covenant in the Holy of Holies.

Yeshua – The Hebrew name of Messiah, transliterated through the Greek as *Jesus*, meaning "the Lord is salvation" or "the Lord saves."

God's Redemptive Program

Feast	Also Known As	Scripture	Fulfillment
Passover	Pesach	Lev. 23:4–5	1 Cor. 5:7
Unleavened Bread	Hag HaMatzot	Lev. 23:6–8	1 Cor. 5:8
Firstfruits	Reishit	Lev. 23:9–14	1 Cor. 15:21–23
Pentecost	Feast of Weeks Shavuot	Lev. 23:15–21	Acts 2:1–10 James 1:18
Feast of Trumpets	Yom HaTeruah Rosh HaShanah	Lev. 23:23–25	1 Cor. 15:52 1 Thess. 4:16–17
Day of Atonement	Yom Kippur	Lev. 23:28–32	Zech. 12:10–13:1 Matt. 23:39
Feast of Tabernacles	Feast of Booths Sukkot	Lev. 23:33–44	Zech. 14:16 Rev. 7:9, 15

Feasts of the Bible Calendar

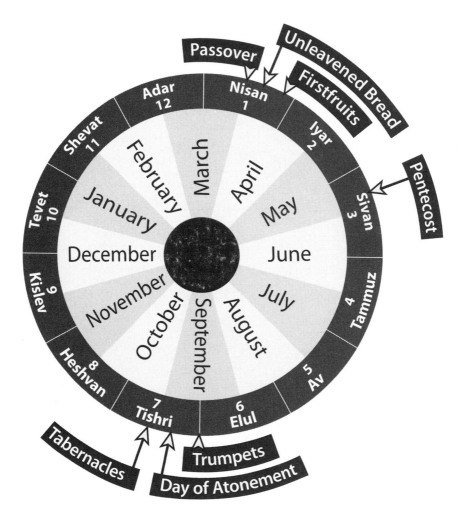

Get into God's Word

Key Bible Verses

Read: Exodus 20:8–11
Study Question: According to this passage, how did people in the Bible keep the Sabbath holy?

_____

_____

_____

Read: Romans 5:1–2
Study Question: How does a person find peace with God?

_____

_____

_____

Read: Hebrews 4:1–11
Study Question: What prevents some people from entering God's rest?

_____

_____

_____

Read: Leviticus 23:1–44
Write down each of the feasts you can identify in this passage and some of the instructions for how each feast should be observed.

_____

_____

_____

_____

_____

_____

Talk about It

Discussion Questions

1. Why did God establish the Sabbath?

   _____

   _____

   _____

2. How does Messiah Jesus fulfill the Sabbath?

   _____

   _____

   _____

3. How can resting from our daily routines of work honor the Lord?

   _____

   _____

   _____

4. What does God want to teach us through dedicating a day to rest in him?

   _____

   _____

   _____

5. After watching this introduction to the seven biblical feasts, what are you most looking forward to learning in the upcoming sessions?

   _____

   _____

   _____

Stop and Pray

Sabbath Prayer

In traditional Jewish households worldwide there is a Sabbath prayer that is chanted by the lady of the home to welcome the Sabbath by lighting the candles. For Jewish people who have accepted Jesus as their Messiah, this traditional Hebrew prayer is modified to honor Jesus in this blessing.

English
Blessed are You, O Lord our God, King of the Universe who has sanctified us through faith in Jesus the Messiah, the Light of the World, and in his name we kindle the Sabbath lights.

Hebrew
Baruch Atah Adonai Eloheinu, Melech Ha'olam, asher kidshanu al yaday emuna b'Yeshua haMashiach, Or HaOlam, oo'b'Shmo anu madlikiim haner shel Shabbat.

Notes:

_____

_____

_____

_____

_____

_____

_____

_____

_____

_____

_____

_____

Think about It

Reflection Questions

1. Read Colossians 2:16–17. Meditate on the liberty that is given to us in Jesus.

   _____

   _____

   _____

   _____

   _____

   _____

2. Take a few minutes to reflect and see if you have set apart a regular time to focus on the Lord. If you do not have a regular time, what do you need to do to find the time?

   _____

   _____

   _____

   _____

   _____

   _____

3. If you already have a weekly meeting with the Lord to reorient your life around his values, how has this changed your priorities?

   _____

   _____

   _____

   _____

   _____

   _____

> *Learn More*

Digging Deeper

1. What does it mean that the Sabbath Day is "holy"?

After creation, God was pleased with all that was done and rested on the seventh day. "Then God blessed the seventh day and made it holy, because on it he rested from all the work of creating that he had done" (Gen. 2:3 NIV). Other English translations say God "sanctified" the seventh day. To sanctify or "to make holy to the Lord" something or someone is to set it apart for God's purposes. In ancient Israel, items set apart for sacred use, such as the altar (Ex. 29:37) and anointing oil (Ex. 30:25), were made holy. People set apart for special purposes, such as the priests (Lev. 21:6) and the nation of Israel (Jer. 2:3), are called holy. Fast forward to the first century; Jesus is said to be sanctified and set apart by God (Heb. 7:26). Believers in Jesus are therefore also considered holy (Eph. 2:21). To be made holy means that God qualifies the person or thing to be used for his purposes, and what God qualifies and sets apart for himself is considered holy and acceptable in his presence.

God instructed his people to keep the seventh day, or Sabbath, holy by remembering his work of creation and relating to him by setting usual business aside. "For six days work may be done, but on the seventh day there is a Sabbath of complete rest, a holy convocation. You shall not do any work; it is a Sabbath to the LORD in all your dwellings" (Lev. 23:3). The point of this command to rest was not simply to avoid work, but to ensure that the holy day is truly set apart for relating to the Lord.

The children of Israel understood that it is not optional to meet with God regularly. God created us for relationship with him, and Sabbath was God's invitation to enter into that relationship. He commanded us as well to abide in him for it is in our best interest to grow in our relationship with him. Jesus told his followers: "Abide in Me, and I in you. As the branch cannot bear fruit of itself unless it abides in the vine, so neither can you unless you abide in Me" (John 15:4).

2. Did Jesus "break" the Sabbath?

Jesus and the religious authorities of his day were not always on the same page when it came to Sabbath observance. In order to understand their disconnect, we need to take a look at how the Pharisees arrived at their religious practices. The Pharisees were respected teachers of the Law of Moses and knew that disobedience to the Law of Moses had a weighty price tag. The Jewish nation was disciplined by the Lord through the Babylonian exile for 70 years. Therefore, the scribes and teachers of Israel tried to prevent such judgment from happening again by developing additional regulations that would serve as a type of "fence" around the Law of Moses. But with this seemingly good idea came the danger of focusing on the "fence" and losing sight of the primary meaning of God's commands, including the meaning of the Sabbath. In Jesus' day, observing all the Sabbath regulations was elevated above other commands such as kindness and charity.

The way Jesus acted on the Sabbath became a point of persecution and even rejection of Jesus as the Messiah of Israel. In Matthew 12, Jesus allows his disciples to pluck the heads of grain to eat on the Sabbath, and he also heals a man with a shriveled hand on the Sabbath. The Pharisees challenged Jesus as to why he allowed his disciples to do what was contrary to the traditions of keeping the Sabbath. (Note that they were not accused of stealing the grain from someone else's field, but of plucking the grain on the Sabbath.) We learn about this provision for the hungry in the Law of Moses in Deuteronomy 23:25. However, Jewish traditions equated plucking ears with reaping grain, which was forbidden on the Sabbath.

Jesus responded to his accusers with another passage in Scripture, 1 Samuel 21:1–6, where David broke the Law when he was hungry and took the bread from the house of God that was set apart for priests only, but he was not condemned. Just as David who was hungry was given bread from the holy place to eat, also, Jesus said that priests break the Sabbath by working in the temple, yet remain innocent. Messiah Jesus is teaching them that something greater than the temple was here, indicating that his own disciples in serving him were as priests serving in the temple. Jesus declares that he is "Lord of the Sabbath." This claim is implicitly messianic, going beyond the mere right to tamper with tradition. It places Jesus in a position to handle the Sabbath law any way that he wills. Jesus is greater than the Law and is therefore qualified to give meaning and definition to Sabbath observance. The authority of the temple laws (like offering the doubled burnt offering on the Sabbath according to Numbers 28:9–10) shielded the priests from being guilty of breaking the Sabbath. Likewise, the authority of Jesus shielded his disciples from guilt. Jesus said that he is greater than the temple. The temple only had merit because of the Lord whom it served. All who serve him are free from restrictions in that service. The law points to Jesus and finds its fulfillment in him (see Matt. 5:17–48).

God is not looking for worshipers who simply follow traditions, but who are motivated by love. Why does God declare that he is indifferent about ceremonies, when he strictly enjoined in his Law that they should be observed? The answer is easy. External rites are of no value in themselves. God desires "compassion and not sacrifice" (Hos. 6:6). Our understanding of the Scriptures should bring us not to judge people, but rather to have compassion and love which are truly at the heart of the Law.

3. **What about other Jewish holidays, such as Purim and Hanukkah? Are they biblical?**

Although other holidays, such as Purim and Hanukkah, are not part of the seven feasts of Leviticus 23, they are biblical and Jesus observed these feasts. He utilized them to point to himself as Messiah of Israel and Savior of the world.

Purim (Feast of Lots) – This holiday's origin can be found in the book of Esther. It commemorates how Queen Esther saved the Jewish people from annihilation while exiled in Persia. Today, Purim is celebrated with carnivals, treats, and a reading of the book of Esther. The story of Esther reminds us that God is faithful to his promises to save those who trust in him.

Hanukkah (Feast of Lights or Feast of Dedication) – This holiday commemorates the rededication of the temple in Jerusalem in the second century BC. A Seleucid king had plundered and defiled the temple, but a Jewish family called the Maccabees led a successful revolt to recover the temple and rededicate it to God. This feast was celebrated in Jesus' day. John 10:22 mentions Jesus being at the temple during the Feast of

Dedication. Today this feast is celebrated with lighting the candles of the Hanukkah menorah and often with giving presents. This holiday reminds us of the importance of remaining faithful to God during persecution.

Passover, Unleavened Bread, and Firstfruits

Our Lamb for Eternity

HINT

Be sure to see the key terms and charts starting on page 29.

Follow Along and Take Notes

Session 2 Outline:
Passover, Unleavened Bread, and Firstfruits

I. Feast of Passover

    A. Head, beginning, foundation

        1. Exodus 12:2

        2. Release from bondage

    B. Feast of Unleavened Bread

    C. Feast of Firstfruits (Reishit)

        1. 1 Corinthians 15:20

        2. Commemorates the death, burial, and resurrection of our Lord

II. Passover Preparation

    A. Jesus celebrated Passover

      1. Luke 22:7–13

B. Two Reasons for Unleavened Bread (Matzah)

      1. Historical Reason

         a) Deuteronomy 16:3

      2. Leaven Pictures Sin

         a) Leviticus 2:11

         b) 1 Corinthians 8:1

         c) 1 Corinthians 5:6–8

         d) 1 John 1:9

C. Elijah Tradition: Herald of the Lord

      1. Malachi 3–4

      2. John the Baptist; John 1:29

D. Four Cups

1. Four-fold blessing of redemption

2. Exodus 6:6–7

III. Passover Service

   A. Lighting of the Candles

   B. Haggadah = "the telling"

      1. Exodus 12:26–27

   C. Seder Plate

      1. Parsley & Salt Water

      2. Bitter Herbs

      3. Charoset

      4. Egg

      5. Shank Bone

   D. First Cup: Consecration

    1. Matzah Tash (Bread Bag) or Echad (Unity)

    2. Triune God of Israel; Isaiah 48:16

E. Second Cup: Plagues (Judgment)

    1. Death of the Firstborn

        a) Exodus 4:22–23

    2. Provision for Our Redemption

        a) Exodus 12:3

        b) Concept of Judgment

    3. Passover Lamb

        a) Zechariah 9:9

    4. Passover Story

        a) Exodus 12:7, 13

        b) Psalm 22; Isaiah 53

 F. Family Meal

  1. Afikomen ("that which comes afterward")

 G. Third Cup: Redemption

  1. The Lord's Supper

   a) Luke 22:19–20

  2. New Covenant

   a) Jeremiah 31:31–34

   b) John 17:3

   c) Revelation 3:20

 H. Fourth Cup: Hallel (Praise)

  1. Elijah's empty seat

  2. Heralds going forth

Key Terms

Afikomen – (Ah-fee-KO-men) broken piece of matzah that is taken out from the second compartment of the matzah bag. It is hidden away until the third cup of the Passover Seder and then redeemed by a child who finds it. *Afikomen* is a Greek word that means "that which comes after." It is this broken matzah that Messiah Jesus utilized to institute what has come to be called The Lord's Supper (Luke 22:19).

Bitter Herbs – One of the three items commanded to be eaten at the first Passover according to Exodus 12:8–9. In Egypt, the bitter herbs were to remind the Israelites that their lives as slaves were full of bitterness. Today, as followers of Jesus, these bitter herbs remind us of the bitterness of our lives when we were slaves to sin.

Elijah's Cup or Cup of Hallel – In the Passover Seder the four cups each have a name. The fourth cup is known as the Cup of Hallel (Praise), but it is also called Elijah's Cup to remember that Elijah's coming would precede the coming of the Messiah. This fourth cup is mentioned in Matthew 26:29–30 when Jesus and his disciples sang a song of praise at the end of the Passover meal.

The Exodus – The story of how God delivered the Israelites from bondage in ancient Egypt by Moses. This account is recorded in the book of Exodus.

Feast of Firstfruits – Also called *Reishit* (Re-SHEET), it was the day of offering the first ripe sheaf (the firstfruits) of barley to the Lord as an act of dedicating the harvest to him. Observed on the third day after Passover (Lev. 23:9–14). Jewish people rarely celebrate Reishit today, but it has great significance for followers of Jesus as the day of his resurrection.

Feast of Unleavened Bread – Also called *Hag HaMatzot* (Hawg Hah-MAHT-zot), in Scripture it is mentioned as a separate feast on the fifteenth day of the same month as Passover (Lev. 23:6–8; Ex. 12:15–20). Today, the feasts of Passover, Unleavened Bread, and Firstfruits have all been incorporated into the eight-day celebration of Passover.

Haggadah – (Ha-GA-dah) means "the telling" and refers to the book used to explain the Seder service.

Leaven – *Chametz* is the Hebrew word for "leaven" which is any food that is made of grain and water that has been allowed to ferment and rise. Leaven is seen as a corrupting agent and is forbidden at Passover time. Leavened bread is the opposite of matzah or unleavened bread.

The Last Supper – Traditional name for the last Passover meal that Messiah Jesus ate with his disciples. In 1 Corinthians 11:20 Paul calls it "the Lord's supper" because at the third cup (Cup of Redemption) Jesus instituted Communion. It is at this cup that Jesus pointed to himself saying, "This cup which is poured out for you is the new covenant in My blood" (Luke 22:20). He also took the Afikomen piece of matzah and referred to his body as a sacrifice (Luke 22:19). Therefore, Communion is a part of God's Passover.

Matzah – The unleavened bread eaten on Passover to recall the haste in which the Israelites left Egypt (Deut. 16:3). It is made with water and flour only, not any leaven, and during the baking process the dough is pierced so it will not fracture into pieces in the oven.

Matzah Tash – This is the matzah bag, also referred to by many Jewish people as the *Echad*, meaning "unity." It contains three compartments with one slice of unleavened bread (matzah) in each compartment. The second compartment contains the Afikomen.

Matzah Tash (Bread Bag)

New Covenant – A biblical term referring to a new kind of relationship between God and humanity in which sins are forgiven and each person can know God personally. This new covenant was foretold by the prophet Jeremiah (Jer. 31:31–34) and promised by Messiah Jesus at the Last Supper. It is through Messiah that this new covenant is instituted.

Pesach – (PAY-sahch) The Hebrew way to say Passover. It comes from a Hebrew root meaning "to pass over." Pesach refers to the fact that God passed over the houses of the Jews when he slew the firstborn of Egypt (Ex. 12:12–13).

Seder – (SAY-der) Hebrew word that means "order" and refers to the order of service for the Passover meal. At each Passover table there is a special Seder plate with various ceremonial foods to be eaten during the meal. Today, a Passover meal can simply be called a Seder or Passover Seder.

Torah – Usually understood as Law, but in Hebrew it literally means "instruction." Consists of the first five books of Moses: Genesis, Exodus, Leviticus, Numbers, and Deuteronomy.

The Four Cups of the Passover Seder

	Cup of...	Meaning	Scripture
1	Consecration (Sanctification)	"I will bring you out"	Exodus 6:6
2	Plagues (Judgment)	"I will deliver you"	Exodus 6:6
3	Redemption	"I will redeem you"	Exodus 6:7
4	Praise (Hallel)	"I will take you for my people"	Exodus 6:7

Seder Plate

Bitter Herbs (Maror)

Egg (Betzah)

Shank Bone (Zeroah)

Parsley (Karpas)*

Charoset

Bitter Herbs (Maror)

*A bowl of salt water is often placed off to the side of the plate in which to dip the parsley.

> *Get into God's Word*

Key Bible Verses

Read: Exodus 12:1–12
Study Question: How did the people of Israel avoid the tenth and most terrible plague?

_____

_____

_____

Read: Leviticus 23:5–14
Study Question: According to this passage, what are do's and don'ts of observing Passover? (The first two are filled in for you.)

v. 6 _Do eat unleavened bread_ _____

v. 7 _Don't do any laborious work_ _____

v. 8–9 _____

v. 10–11 _____

v. 12 _____

v. 13 _____

v. 14 _____

Read: Matthew 26:1–5, 17–30
Study Question: During this Passover meal, what did Jesus reveal to his disciples about who he was and what was going to happen?

_____

_____

_____

Read: 1 Corinthians 5:6–8
Study Question: What (or who) is the "old leaven" Paul instructs believers to remove?

_____

_____

_____

Talk about It

Discussion Questions

I.   Have you participated in a Passover Seder? If so, share your experience
     of it with the group.

     _____

     _____

2.   What is the significance of beginning the biblical year with the Feast
     of Passover?

     _____

     _____

     _____

3.   Why was it important for each family to apply the blood of the lamb to
     their doorway?

     _____

     _____

     _____

4.   What if a religious Jewish family decided they did not want to apply the
     lamb's blood to their door? Would they have escaped judgment? (See
     Ex. 12:7, 12–13)

     _____

     _____

5.   There are many symbolic elements and set practices in a Passover Seder.
     What are some of the benefits of having symbols and ceremonies in
     worship? What are some of the possible pitfalls?

     _____

     _____

     _____

Stop and Pray

Passover Prayer

The Passover Seder is led by the head of the household, the father or the grandfather of the family. However, the woman of the household has the privilege to welcome this celebration by lighting the candles and reciting a Passover blessing. The blessing below is modified from the traditional Jewish blessing to reflect Jesus as the Light of world.

English
Blessed are You, O Lord our God, king of the universe who sanctified us through faith in Messiah, Jesus, the Light of the world and it's in his name that we kindle the Passover lights, amen.

Hebrew
Baruch Atah Adonai Eloheinu, Melech Ha'olam, asher kidshanu al yaday emuna b'Yeshua haMashiach, Or HaOlam, oo'b'Shmo anu madlikiim haner shel Pasach.

Notes:

Reflection Questions

1. Read and reflect on the progressive revelation that God gave us concerning the Lamb.

    - A lamb for the person – Genesis 22:7

    - A lamb for the family – Exodus 12:13

    - A lamb for Israel – Isaiah 53

    - A lamb for the world – John 1:29

    - A lamb for eternity – Revelation 5:5

    _____

    _____

    _____

    _____

2. Write down several ways that having a "Lamb for eternity" can impact your life today in how you use your time, your talents, and your resources.

    _____

    _____

    _____

    _____

    _____

    _____

    _____

    _____

    _____

Learn More

Going Deeper

1. **Why did God require a bloody sacrifice—the killing of a lamb—to spare the people?**

In the Bible, we read about people routinely sacrificing animals in obedience to God's commands. Why did God require all the bloody sacrifices? The Scriptures are clear. It states in Leviticus 17:11, "For the life of the flesh is in the blood, and I have given it to you on the altar to make atonement for your souls; for it is the blood by reason of the life that makes atonement."

The annual Passover lambs that were sacrificed pointed to the necessity of substitutionary sacrifices. Substitutionary sacrifices are those offerings that God accepted in the place of the sinner (Lev. 1–5). These sacrifices were presented day after day and year after year, in order to attain forgiveness of sins. Each person that brought a sin offering as the payment for sin had to identify with the innocence of the animal offered, and then by placing his hands on that animal, transferring the sin as an exchange, killing it in front of the priest. This is the essence of identification with the sacrifice and forgiveness of sins that the shedding of blood brings. This is why, in the first Passover in Egypt, God required placing the blood on the door; each family placed the blood on their door by faith. God is looking to redeem people of faith who would trust in his way of redemption and follow him completely. The death of each family's Passover lamb must have been personal and even traumatic because for four days the year-old lamb lived with the family—becoming a part of the family. In Exodus 12, we notice that Moses wrote precise instruction about this lamb using different articles. The articles go from *a* lamb, to *the* lamb, and finally to *your* lamb. Note the progression of the family's identification with the Lamb.

> Exodus 12:3 "they are each one to take a lamb for themselves"
> Exodus 12:4 "...you are to divide the lamb."
> Exodus 12:5 "*Your* lamb shall be..."

Each family went from selecting *a* lamb from many lambs, and once this lamb was selected it became *the* lamb. After the lamb was inspected and deemed to be without blemish it became *their* lamb for sacrifice and its blood was applied to the door of the home—a personal sacrifice to redeem them from slavery. After having this little lamb in their home they would have become attached to it. Can you imagine their sense of guilt when eating this meat? There was a personal identification with this lamb.

This sacrifice foreshadowed a coming and final substitutionary sacrifice, the Messiah, the Lamb of God. It is personal identification with the Lamb of God through faith that spares us from judgment.

2. **How do Jesus' last days mirror the celebration of Passover?**

Palm Sunday. It began with Jesus' entry into Jerusalem on the colt of a donkey, which is commonly known as the triumphal entry on Palm Sunday (Mark 11:1–11). This Sunday would have been the 10th of the month when each family who had come up to Jerusalem to celebrate Passover would be selecting a lamb for sacrifice.

Inspected. From this 10th day until the 14th day of the month Jesus was tested by all the authorities of the day: civil, political, and religious (See Luke 20:1–8, 19–26, 27–47; 22:54, 66–71). He was found truly to be without spot and without blemish as a Roman official declared to all, "I find no fault in Him" (Luke 23:4). Passover lambs had to be unblemished (Ex. 12:5).

Passover Meal. Jesus partook of the Passover meal with his disciples on the first night of Passover on the 14th of Nisan, the same night when all Israel would be partaking of their lambs.

Sacrifice. Later that night after Judas betrayed him, Jesus was arrested in the middle of the night, and died on the first day of Passover (Luke 22).

No Broken Bone. John 19:36 points out that not a single bone of Jesus was broken—neither during the course of the beatings nor by the Roman soldiers who broke the legs of the other men crucified alongside Jesus. Similarly, the Jewish people were to be careful to make sure that not a single bone of the Passover lamb was broken (See Ex. 12:8–9, 46; Ps. 22:17).

3. What is the difference between the Passover meal and the Lord's Supper?

The Lord's Supper (or Communion) was a practice Jesus instituted during the last Passover meal he celebrated with his disciples before his death. He gave new meaning to the Passover elements.

In Luke 22:19 Jesus identifies himself with the Passover bread. Messiah Jesus took the bread and said, "This is My body which is given for you; do this in remembrance of Me." This bread is called the Afikomen, the broken piece of matzah (unleavened bread) that had been hidden away. Messiah taught his disciples that this matzah represents his sacrifice for he is truly the only sinless, unleavened, perfect Lamb of God.

Luke 22:20 reads, "And in the same way He took the cup after they had eaten, saying, 'This cup which is poured out for you is the new covenant in My blood.'" This cup was the third cup of wine which is traditionally called the Cup of Redemption. It is taken after the meal. Notice how Jesus gave this cup a new meaning by telling his followers that this cup was the "new covenant." His disciples would have been familiar with the promise of the new covenant from the prophet Jeremiah: "'Behold, days are coming,' declares the LORD, 'when I will make a new covenant with the house of Israel and with the house of Judah, not like the covenant which I made with their fathers in the day I took them by the hand to bring them out of the land of Egypt.... I will put My law within them and on their heart I will write it; and I will be their God, and they shall be My people'" (Jer. 31:31–33).

Therefore, Communion or the Lord's Supper is a part of Passover. Every year when we celebrate the Passover deliverance, we who trust in Jesus the Messiah don't stop at the borders of Egypt, but rather remember our perfect Lamb who redeemed us from the slavery of sin and death.

Pentecost

The Birthday of the Body of Messiah

HINT

Be sure to see the key terms and charts starting on page 43.

Follow Along and Take Notes

Session 3 Outline: *Pentecost*

I.   Pentecost (Shavuot/Feast of Weeks)

    A.   Acts 2

        1.   3,000 baptized; Acts 2:41

        2.   "fully come" = fulfillment; Acts 2:1; Luke 8:23

        3.   Formation of the Body of Messiah

    B.   Season of the Giving of the Law

        1.   Exodus 19:1

        2.   Season of the Giving of the Spirit

        3.   Noise and fire

            a)   Exodus 19:18–19

            b)   Acts 2:2–3

4. Golden calf

5. 3,000 died; 3,000 lived

    a)   Exodus 32:28

    b)   Acts 2:41

6. Law shows God's holiness, our sin

II. Pentecost Reveals the Messiah

    1. Leviticus 23:15

    2. Leviticus 23:16–17

A. Second Firstfruits

    1. Barley harvest; wheat harvest

    2. Believers are firstfruits

        a)   James 1:17–18

B. Dateless feast

      1. Shavuot = "weeks"

      2. Count 50 days from Passover

C. Pentecost Offering

      1. Two loaves (Leviticus 23:17)

          a) Two witnesses (Deuteronomy 19:15)

          b) Disciples sent out by two (Mark 6:7)

          c) Jews and Gentiles (Deuteronomy 16:16; Acts 2:10)

      2. Leaven (chametz)

          a) Leviticus 23:17

          b) Come as you are

      3. Fine flour (solet)

          a) Refined, crushed

          b) Conforming us to him

Key Terms

Body of Messiah – A term for all those who have trusted in Jesus as their Savior through his blood atonement. Messiah is called the head and believers are the body (Eph. 4:15–16). Until Pentecost was fulfilled, the Holy Spirit came upon individuals for a period of time to accomplish the task God called them to fulfill (for example, Judg. 3:10; Ex. 31:3). But now since the outpouring of the Holy Spirit at Pentecost in Acts 2, every believer who comes to the saving knowledge of Jesus is permanently indwelt by the Holy Spirit. Therefore, the Body of Messiah is a community of redeemed people indwelt by the Spirit.

Firstfruits – The first and best of the agricultural offering presented to the Lord.

Gentile – A non-Jew or non-Israelite. In Hebrew the term for Gentile is goy and the plural is *goyim* which is a biblical term for the nations.

Leaven – *Chametz* is the Hebrew term for "leaven" which is any food that is made of grain and water that has been allowed to ferment and rise. In Scripture, leaven is a corrupting agent that pictures sin.

Mosaic Law – The law that, according to the Old Testament, God gave to the Israelites through Moses. The Mosaic Law contains 613 commandments including many rules of religious observance given in the first five books of the Old Testament. In Judaism, these five books are called the Torah, or the Law.

Pilgrimage Feasts – In the Bible (Deut. 16:16–17) God commands all Israelites to appear before him or "come up to Jerusalem" three times a year: at Passover (the Feast of Unleavened Bread), Pentecost, and the Feast of Tabernacles.

Proselyte – This biblical term comes from both the Greek and Hebrew idea for a "stranger," a "newcomer to Israel," or a "sojourner in the land." In the rabbinical writings and in the New Testament, it is used for a convert to Judaism from paganism.

Shavuot – (Sha-voo-OTE) Hebrew word meaning "weeks." Also called Feast of Weeks, Pentecost (from the Greek word for "fifty"), and the Season of the Giving of the Law. It is celebrated on the 50th day after Passover.

Ruach HaKodesh – Hebrew for the Holy Spirit. *Ruach* literally means "spirit," *Ha* means "the," and *Kodesh* means "holy." Biblically, the Holy Spirit is the third Person of the Trinity, who indwells each person who receives Jesus as his or her personal Savior.

Solet – (so-LET) Hebrew for "fine flour" that has been stripped and crushed to remove the inconsistencies and lumps. In Leviticus 23:17 it describes the flour that made up the two-loaf offering for Pentecost.

Torah – Hebrew word meaning "instruction," translated as Law. This divine instruction refers to the Five Books of Moses: Genesis, Exodus, Leviticus, Numbers, and Deuteronomy.

Firstfruits Comparison

Firstfruits during Passover	Firstfruits during Pentecost
Spring barley harvest	Summer wheat harvest
Presented the day after the Sabbath of Passover Week.	Presented 50 days after Passover.
Pictures Messiah as our firstfruits from the dead (1 Cor. 15:21–23).	Pictures believers as the firstfruits of Messiah's new creation, the "body" of Messiah (Acts 2).
Bread made without leaven.	Two loaves made with leaven.
Meaning: Jesus is the acceptable and perfect sacrifice.	Meaning: Believers are accepted by God because Jesus was accepted by his Father as a perfect sacrifice for our sins.

Giving of the Law and Spirit Comparison

Giving of the Law	Giving of the Spirit
Exodus 19:1–20:20; 32	Acts 2
Spiritual birthday of Israel	Spiritual birthday of the body of Messiah
Traditionally believed to have happened about 50 days after the Israelites left Egypt (Ex. 19:1)	Believers in Jesus were gathered together on the day of Pentecost, 50 days after they celebrated Passover.
Fire and noise as God descended Mt. Sinai (Ex. 19:16–18).	A violent, rushing wind and tongues as fire descended upon the believers.
3,000 people died because of their idolatry (Ex. 32:28).	3,000 people were made spiritually alive because they believed in Jesus.
Law given to instruct the Israelites.	Spirit given to empower and guide the body of Messiah—including both Jews and Gentiles.

Get into God's Word

Key Bible Verses

Read: Leviticus 23:15–22
Study Question: There are many instructions for this feast in the Bible. Write down all the aspects of this feast that you can find in this passage of Scripture.

_____

_____

_____

_____

_____

_____

Read: Acts 2:1–41
Study Question: When the believers in Jesus were filled with the Holy Spirit, what were the different responses from the crowd?

_____

_____

_____

_____

_____

Read: James 1:17–18
Study Question: According to this passage, what does it mean that we as believers are "firstfruits"?

_____

_____

_____

_____

_____

_____

Discussion Questions

1. Why is there an emphasis on counting 50 days to determine the date of the observance of Pentecost?

    _____

    _____

    _____

2. What is the significance of the two loaves that had to be presented for this feast?

    _____

    _____

    _____

3. What is the importance of the two loaves being made with leaven, and why was this unusual offering only accepted on the day of Pentecost?

    _____

    _____

    _____

4. What Scriptures come to mind when you think of giving your first and your best (your "firstfruits") to God in your relationship and your service to him?

    _____

    _____

    _____

5. What questions do you still have about the Feast of Pentecost?

    _____

    _____

    _____

Stop and Pray

Prayer over Bread

This ancient Jewish blessing is recited before partaking of bread products.

English
Blessed are you, O Lord our God, King of the universe, who brings forth bread from the ground.

Hebrew
Baruch Atah Adonai Eloheinu Melech ha'olam hamotzi lechem min ha'arets.

Notes:

Think about It

Reflection Questions

1. Imagine if you were there at the foot of the Mount Sinai when the Law was given. Think how terrifying it must have been first to witness Moses coming down the mountain from the presence of the Lord and then to be found guilty of idolatry and deserving of judgment and death. Then imagine the striking contrast of being with the disciples of Jesus in the temple when the Holy Spirit was given. Take a minute to thank God for his grace that has been poured out on you through the redemption of Jesus, the gift of salvation!

    _____

    _____

    _____

2. In Jewish tradition there is a custom to read the book of Ruth during Pentecost because Ruth's redemption story took place during harvest time and features the Pentecost portion from Leviticus 23:22. Take some time this week to read the book of Ruth. Reflect on how God redeemed Ruth the Moabite and how through Ruth's testimony her bitter mother-in-law was restored back to the God of Israel. Can you think of how God used your faithfulness (or the faithfulness of someone you know) to restore another believer back to the Lord?

    _____

    _____

    _____

3. Leaven is seen as a corrupting agent, but it is allowed in the Pentecost offering. How does this leaven in the offering display God's mercy and acceptance of each of us as sinners? How does this teach us to love and accept others in the body of Messiah?

    _____

    _____

    _____

> *Learn More*

Going Deeper

1. **In Scripture, there are different kinds of offerings for Pentecost. What is the difference between the types of offerings in the Bible?**

The sacrificial offerings in Leviticus were all meant to point to the Messiah and his fulfillment of them. The heart of the gospel is that Jesus died for our sins. But in order to appreciate his sacrifice on our behalf we need to understand what these offerings represented. The word for offerings or sacrifices in Hebrew is *korbanot*. The root of this word means "to draw near" and indicates the primary goal of these sacrifices: to draw near to God. God is holy; therefore we can only draw near to him according to his appointed sacrifices.

Sin Offering: The Hebrew word is *chatat* meaning "to sin." This offering was the basis of all offerings and it was the most important of all the sacrifices. The sin offering symbolized redemption or atonement for the wrongs the people had committed. Because atonement is foundational to restoring relationship with God, the sin offering was the sacrifice that made all the other offerings possible. Messiah Jesus who was sinless himself became the once-for-all sin offering for us: "[God] made Him who knew no sin to be sin [offering] on our behalf, so that we might become the righteousness of God in Him" (2 Cor. 5:21).

Burnt offering or whole offering: The Hebrew word is *olah*, meaning "going up" or "ascension." *Olah* offering was completely burnt on the altar; no part was eaten by anyone. This offering represented complete submission to God's will and dedication to God; therefore the entire offering was given to God. The apostle Paul teaches how Jesus was that burnt offering as he totally gave himself as a sacrifice to God, a fragrant aroma. Burnt offering is that fragrant aroma of total surrender and dedication that brings delight to the heart of God. "Therefore be imitators of God, as beloved children; and walk in love, just as Christ also loved you and gave himself up for us, an offering and a sacrifice to God as a fragrant aroma" (Eph. 5:1–2).

The grain offering: The Hebrew word is *mincha* and refers to an offering from the produce of the ground. Grain was the staple of people's diets, and unlike today, most physical sustenance and nourishment came from grain. Therefore, it represented dependence on God to provide rain and favorable climate to produced bountiful harvest as well as health and strength to be able to toil in the fields. This grain offering points to Messiah's perfect life and ministry and how he went about his Father's business. He was able to say, "It is finished" and report to the Father that he completed the work he came to do. Jesus said, "I am the bread of life; he who comes to Me will not hunger" (John 6:35).

The Peace Offering: The Hebrew word is *zebach sh'lamim* which comes from the word *shalom,* meaning "peace" or "wholeness" or "completeness." The peace offering brings restoration and peace with God. It is through this offering that the fellowship between humanity and God is restored. This particular offering was burned on the altar, a portion was given to the priests, and the rest was eaten by the person making the offering and his family. The peace offering is fulfilled in Messiah, who became our peace offering, reconciling us with God and with one another. "But now in Christ Jesus you who once were far away have been brought near by the blood of Christ. For he himself is our peace [offering], who has made the two groups one and has destroyed the barrier, the dividing wall of hostility" (Eph. 2:13–14).

2. **What does it mean to be "firstfruits"?**

All believers from the day of Pentecost (Acts 2) until now are the firstfruits of Messiah's work. The firstfruits of Passover point to Messiah as the firstfruits from the dead; the firstfruits of Pentecost point to the harvest of his labor. All believers together are the result of his complete work of redemption. Firstfruits conveys the idea that everything belongs to God. Presenting the firstfruits offering was a way of acknowledging and giving thanks to the Lord as the provider of all things.

In Romans 8:23 Paul says, "And not only this, but also we ourselves, having the first fruits of the Spirit, even we ourselves groan within ourselves, waiting eagerly for our adoption as sons, the redemption of our body." In this verse, Paul is assuring us that the indwelling of the Holy Spirit of God is a guarantee or surety that our earthly bodies will be eternally redeemed. In other words, having the Holy Spirit in our lives is a pledge or down payment upon all the future promises that will be ultimately fulfilled when we reach our eternal home in heaven.

Just as Jesus was accepted as the firstfruits of Passover, so we are accepted by God as the firstfruits of Pentecost. Therefore we are to live out that acceptance and love of God, having confidence that we are dedicated to God's use only. When we put God first in our lives we testify to the world that we belong to him.

Feast of Trumpets

Getting Ready for the Gathering

4

HINT

Be sure to see the key terms and charts starting on page 57.

Follow Along and Take Notes

Session 4 Outline: *Feast of Trumpets*

I. Three Fall Feasts

    A. Feast of Trumpets (Yom HaTeruah)

    B. Day of Atonement (Yom Kippur)

    C. Tabernacles (Sukkot)

II. Feast of Trumpets

    A. Sheva = seven, vow

    B. Yom HaTeruah; Rosh HaShanah

    C. Shofar = ram's horn

    D. Silver Trumpets

        1. Numbers 10:1–10

2. Temple Tax; Exodus 30:13

III. Rosh HaShanah (New Year's)

   A. Tishri = "beginnings"

   B. Apples, Honey, Challah

   C. Book of Life

      1. Nehemiah 8:10

   D. High Holy Days

   E. Synagogue Service: Kingship, Remembrance, Shofarot (Trumpets)

IV. Yom Hadin (Day of Judgment)

   A. Tashlich

      1. Micah 7:19

  B. Three Books

    1. Utterly Wicked

    2. Absolutely Righteous

    3. "Tweeners"

  C. Books will be opened

    1. Daniel 7:10

    2. Revelation 20:12

    3. John 5:24

  D. Trumpet blown anytime

    1. Twofold application: Warning, Assembly

    2. Last trumpet; 1 Corinthians 15:15–52

Key Terms

Apples and Honey – Traditional foods eaten on Rosh HaShanah to look forward to the sweetness of a new year (see Neh. 8:10).

Babylonian Captivity (Exile) – The time when Babylon forcibly deported Jews from Judea and Israel to live in Babylonian territories beginning in the late sixth century bc. During exile from their homeland, the Jewish people adopted some Babylonian ways of life, including the Babylonian calendar and new year. This is why the first month of the Jewish civil calendar today is actually the seventh month of the biblical calendar.

Book of Life – Biblically, this is referred to as "the book of the living." Every person born into this world is recorded in the Book of Life (Ps. 139:16). Sin removes us from the Book of Life (Ex. 32:33). Those who believe on the Messiah have their names retained in the Book of Life according to Revelation 3:5; 13:8. (See *Three Books*)

Challah (HA-lah) A braided bread eaten on Sabbath and Jewish holidays. On Rosh HaShanah the bread is made into a circular shape representing the cycle of a new year.

Challah for Rosh HaShanah

Day of Judgment – In Hebrew, *Yom Hadin*, (also called Ten Days of Repentance) a Jewish tradition that teaches that on the Feast of Trumpets (Rosh HaShanah) all Jews are being judged as to whether or not their sins will be forgiven.

Days of Awe – In Hebrew, *Yamin Noraim*. It is the most serious season in the Jewish calendar. This period begins at Rosh HaShanah and includes ten days of introspection and repentance, leading to Yom Kippur on the tenth day. It is a time of soul searching and of making things right with God and one's neighbors.

Fall Feasts – The three biblical holidays that occur in autumn: Feast of Trumpets, Day of Atonement, and Feast of Tabernacles.

High Holy Days – The holidays of Rosh HaShanah and Yom Kippur. The observance of the High Holy Days includes the Days of Awe.

Rosh HaShanah –Jewish New Year, also a traditional name for the Feast of Trumpets.

Sheva – Hebrew word for the number seven. It means "completion," as seven days make a complete week. This same word *sheva* also means "oath" or "vow." For example, the name Elizabeth in Hebrew is *Eli-sheva*, meaning "the oath of God."

Shofar – (SHO-far) The ram's horn trumpet blown on Rosh HaShanah.

Tashlich – (Tash-LIK) Jewish tradition taken from Micah 7:18–20 which prophesied the casting of sins into the depths of the sea. This tradition began in the fifteenth century and is still practiced today in the observant Jewish community. On the afternoon of Rosh HaShanah, families toss bread crumbs into a body of water symbolizing the desire to shed their sins. The crumbs disappearing in the water picture how sins can be taken away, never to return.

Shofar

Talmud – Completed around AD 600, it is a collection of ancient Jewish commentaries which contain the rabbinical comments on the Old Testament from before the time of Jesus and after the time of Jesus. Traditional Judaism holds these codified remarks by various rabbis as authoritative, equal to, or even superior to the Scriptures. During the earthly ministry of Jesus these rabbinical ideas taken from the Talmud put the religious leaders in direct opposition to what Jesus taught. Jewish believers in Messiah Jesus recognize the Bible as the only authoritative source of inspiration.

The Three Books – Jewish tradition teaches that during the Days of Awe three books are opened. One book is for the absolutely wicked; their names will not be written in the Book of Life for the coming year. Another book is for the perfectly righteous; their names will be written in the Book of Life for the coming year. Finally, the third book is opened for those not in either of the first two books, those ordinary people who are neither perfectly evil nor perfectly good. They have to do good works during the ten days of awe in order to include their names in the coming year. (It is important to note that in Judaism often when people speak about being written in the Book of Life, they are referring to physical life and not spiritual life or being saved.)

Tishri – Babylonian word for "beginnings," it is the seventh month of the biblical year and the first month of the Jewish year.

Yom Teruah (Yom HaTeruah) – (YOM True-ah) Hebrew name for the Feast of Trumpets, literally means the "day of blowing."

The Three Fall Feasts

Feast	Meaning	Fulfillment
Feast of Trumpets	Gathering of the Body of Messiah	1 Cor. 15:52
Day of Atonement	Gathering of Israel	Zech. 12:10–13:1
Feast of Tabernacles	Gathering of the Nations	Zech. 14:16; Rev. 9:9, 15

The Three Parts of the Rosh HaShanah Synagogue Service

The synagogue service during Rosh HaShanah includes three fundamental sections. Each section contains selective responsive readings from Scripture. Jewish believers in Jesus add readings from the New Testament, as it points to fulfillment of the Old Testament.

Section	Meaning	Scripture
Malkiyot (Kingship)	God's sovereign rule over his creation. He is Master and King over all the earth and all belongs to him.	Ps. 24 1 Tim. 6:15–16
Zikhronot (Remembrance)	God is a God who remembers his covenants and promises to Israel. He will keep his promises to all who trust in him as well.	Mic. 7:18–20 Rom. 8:1, 3–39
Shofarot (Trumpets)	The shofar is blown to bring to memory God's provision of the ram that Abraham sacrificed in place of his only son, Isaac. There are four types of blasts during this section: 1. Tekiah – Single long blast that symbolizes the expression of joy. 2. Shevarim – Three short blasts that symbolize weeping. 3. Truah – An extremely short blast that symbolizes sorrow. 4. Tekiah Gadolah – Greatest and longest blast that symbolizes the hope of redemption. Also known as the last trump in the New Testament.	Ps. 47:6 Ps. 81:4–5 Ps. 98:6 Isa. 18:3 Matt. 24:31 1 Cor. 15:51–52 1 Thess. 4:16–18

Get into God's Word

Key Bible Verses

Read: Leviticus 23:23–25
Study Question: What are the three biblical requirements for this feast?

_____

_____

_____

_____

_____

_____

_____

Read: Revelation 20:11–15
Study Question: What happens to people whose names are not written in the Book of Life?

_____

_____

_____

_____

_____

_____

Read: 1 Corinthians 15:51–58
Study Question: What is in store for those who trust in Messiah Jesus?

_____

_____

_____

_____

_____

_____

Talk about It

Discussion Questions

1. What is the biblical meaning of the number seven?

    _____

    _____

    _____

    _____

2. What are the three "gatherings" of the three fall feasts? In your own words, what do the gatherings mean?

    _____

    _____

    _____

    _____

    _____

3. How do we get to have our name inscribed in the Lamb's Book of Life?

    _____

    _____

    _____

    _____

4. How does the Jewish tradition about the books that are opened, differ or agree with the Scriptures? In light of this, how can you pray more effectively and specifically for Jewish people?

    _____

    _____

    _____

    _____

> *Think about It*

Reflection Questions

1. Reflect on how God's love for you is displayed in Jesus when he died for you on the cross and took the judgment that you deserved.

_____

_____

_____

_____

_____

_____

2. Contemplate on the return of Jesus when he will usher us into his kingdom. If he came today would you welcome his return? Why or why not?

_____

_____

_____

_____

_____

_____

_____

3. Read Psalm 103. How does God deal with your sins?

_____

_____

_____

_____

_____

_____

Stop and Pray

Rosh HaShanah Prayers

The High Holy Days are filled with liturgical prayers. There is a prayer recited by Jewish believers on the eve of Rosh HaShanah as candles are kindled by the lady of the house at the beginning of the meal. Since apples and honey are such important symbols of Jewish New Year, there is a traditional blessing over the apples and honey.

English
Blessed are You, O Lord our God, King of Universe, Who has sanctified us in Messiah Yeshua, and instructed us to be a light to the world.

Hebrew
Baruch Atah Adonai, Elohaynu Melech ha-olam, Asher kid'shanu B'Mashiach Yeshua, v'tzivanu l'hiyot ohr la-olam. Amen.

English
Blessed are You, O Lord, our God, King of the universe, Who creates the fruit of the tree.

Hebrew
Baruch Atah Adonai Elohaynu Melech ha-olam, boray p'ri ha-aytz.

Notes:

_____

_____

_____

_____

_____

_____

_____

_____

_____

Learn More

Going Deeper

1. What is the significance of the trumpets being silver?

There are two types of trumpets mentioned in the Bible: the ram's horn and the silver trumpets. For example, Joshua and the Israelites blew the ram's horns at Jericho (Josh. 6:4), and when David brought the ark of the covenant to Jerusalem he did so with celebration and the "soundings of ram's horns" (1 Chron. 15:28). We find the instructions for the silver trumpets in Numbers 10. "The LORD spoke further to Moses, saying, 'Make yourself two trumpets of silver, of hammered work you shall make them; and you shall use them for summoning the congregation and for having the camps set out'" (Num. 10:1–2).

Why was silver used? It is likely that the silver used to make the trumpets came from the temple tax or the silver half shekel that all redeemed people had to pay. "This is what everyone who is numbered shall give: half a shekel according to the shekel of the sanctuary (the shekel is twenty gerahs), half a shekel as a contribution to the LORD" (Ex. 30:13). This payment demonstrated that they had been ransomed by the Lord from bondage.

It is important to understand that no one could buy his own redemption; therefore, the half shekel was a memorial to remind them of their redemption before God. Thus whenever the silver trumpets were blown, either for assembly, for alarm, for worship, or for war, the redeemed of the Lord would respond.

The silver trumpets were used primarily in the temple. When the temple was destroyed by the Roman army in AD 70, the use of much of the temple paraphernalia, including the silver trumpets, was discontinued. The shofar (ram's horn) became the trumpet of choice for the Feast of Trumpets. That is why today the shofar is the most common instrument for Rosh HaShanah.

2. Are the Days of Awe a biblical observance?

Since there is little instruction in Leviticus 23 about the Feast of Trumpets, over the years Jewish sages have added traditions as they sought to find ways to draw near to God. One of those observances is known as the Days of Awe. This period consists of ten days of introspection and repentance, leading to Yom Kippur on the tenth day. It is a time of soul searching and of making things right with God and one's neighbors.

Tradition holds that during these days three books are open in heaven and God's judgment is rendered to determine a person's fate. One book is for the absolutely wicked; their names will not be written in the Book of Life for the coming year. Another book is for the perfectly righteous; their names will be written in the Book of Life for the coming year. Finally, the third book is opened for those not in either of the first two books, those ordinary people who are neither perfectly evil nor perfectly good. They have to do good works during the ten days of awe in order to include their names in the coming year.

Although this idea of three books is mere legend that has been greatly embellished, the idea of a book of life has its roots in Scripture. Moses, when he interceded on behalf of rebellious Israel, pleaded with the Lord, "But now, if You will, forgive their sin—and if not, please blot me out from Your book which You have written!" The Lord replied, "Whoever has sinned against Me, I will blot him out of My book" (Ex. 32:32–33). Likewise, David wrote in Psalm 69:28, "May they be blotted out of the book of life and may they not be recorded with the righteous." Daniel, when he was receiving the vision of future escape from judgment, wrote, "And there will be a time of distress such as never occurred since there was a nation until that time; and at that time your people, everyone who is found written in the book, will be rescued" (Dan. 12:1).

In the New Testament Paul refers to the Book of Life (Phil. 4:3). John in Revelation gives additional insight into the books in heaven (also noted in Dan. 7:10) where books will be used at the final judgment to separate the righteous and the wicked for their respective eternal destinies (Rev. 20:12–15; 21:27).

The Days of Awe are the days of solemn personal evaluation of one's soul before God. We are to seek the Lord with all our hearts and his forgiveness of sins. In traditional Judaism, the idea of being written in the Book of Life has to do with physical life and not the idea of being saved; merits in the Days of Awe are believed to be acceptable before God to give people another year. But the Bible teaches us that it is the finished work of Messiah on the cross that makes us accepted before God through the forgiveness of sins.

Day of Atonement

Entering the Presence of God

5

HINT

Be sure to see the key terms and charts starting on page 71.

Follow Along and Take Notes

Session 5 Outline: *Day of Atonement*

I. Day of Atonement (Yom Kippur)

    A. Ten Days of Awe

    B. Leviticus 23:27–32

    C. Kippur = "covering"

    D. Hayom = "the day"

    E. Shabbat Shabbaton (Sabbath of Sabbaths)

        1. Matthew 11:28

II. Tabernacle/Temple

    A. Holy of Holies

    B. Holy Place

    C. Mercy Seat

III. Special Sacrifices

    A. Detailed order of sacrifice

        1. Leviticus 16

    B. Two goats

        1. Azazel (scapegoat)

        2. Two aspects of atonement

    C. Scapegoat legend

        1. No longer any offering

        2. Hebrews 10:18

IV. Identify with the Day

    A. Tallit (prayer robe)

        1. Identify with atonement

    B. Repentance and humility

        1. Identify the need for forgiveness

  C. Blood offering

        1. Leviticus 17:11

        2. Sin separates; Isaiah 59:1–2

  D. Humbling of our souls

        1. Fasting from sin

        2. Isaiah 58

        3. Ephesians 2:8–9

        4. Identify with the work of God in Messiah

        5. Turn from sin to the Savior

  E. Believers observed the Day

        1. Acts 27:9

        2. 1 Corinthians 16:8

Key Terms

Ark of the Covenant – Item in the Holy of Holies of the tabernacle/temple in the shape of a rectangular box, which was gold inside and out. It contained manna, Aaron's rod, and the tablets of the Law.

Ark of the Covenant

Atonement – The covering over of sin; the reconciliation between God and humanity. The final atonement was made by Jesus on behalf of sinners to bring peace between humanity and God through his death on the cross. Jesus became our sin offering. The concept of atonement spans both the Testaments, everywhere pointing to the death, burial, and resurrection of Jesus for the sins of the world.

Azazel – This unique term means "removal" and refers to the goat that was chosen by lot to be sent out into the wilderness, signifying that God removed the sins of the nation of Israel on the Day of Atonement.

Azazel, the Scapegoat

Book of Life – Biblically, this is referred to as "the book of the living." Every person born into this world is recorded in the Book of Life (Ps. 139:16). Sin removes us from the Book of Life (Ex. 32:33). Those who believe on the Messiah have their names retained in the Book of Life according to Revelation 3:5; 13:8.

Days of Awe – In Hebrew *Yamin Noraim* (also called the Ten Days of Repentance), it is the most serious season in the Jewish calendar. This period begins at Rosh HaShanah that includes ten days of introspection and repentance, leading to Yom Kippur on the tenth day. It is a time of soul searching and of making things right with God and one's neighbors.

Destruction of the Temple (AD 70) – Roman military commander Titus led the assault on Jerusalem to quell a Jewish uprising in the First Jewish-Roman War (AD 66–70). In AD 70 the Roman army looted and set fire to Jerusalem and destroyed the temple. Since the destruction of the temple, there has been no acceptable place for blood sacrifice. All that remains today of the structure is a remnant of the wall, known as the Western Wall, which surrounded the temple's courtyard.

Fall Feasts – The three biblical feasts that occur in autumn: Feast of Trumpets, Day of Atonement, and Feast of Tabernacles.

The Fast – Another name for the Day of Atonement. This Day was not a festive assembly, but rather a day of humbling one's soul. Although the Bible does not command fasting on the Day of Atonement, it does say to humble oneself before the Lord. Jewish sages implemented fasting on this day as an expression of humility and affliction. New Testament believers kept this tradition even after Jesus ascended (see Acts 27:9).

High Priest – In Hebrew *cohen gadol*, the chief among the priests. The first was Aaron and all later high priests (and other priests) were required to be descended from Aaron of the tribe of Levi. The high priest was distinguished from the other priests mainly by being permitted to enter the Holy of Holies once a year on the Day of Atonement. Only the high priest had oil poured over his head, in contrast to ordinary priests who were just sprinkled with oil. The high priest's garments also were different from regular priests. He served as a mediator between God and the people, representing the people before God with sacrifice and intercession.

Holy of Holies – Innermost room in the tabernacle/temple, only 15 square feet, containing the Ark of the Covenant. The Holy Place (a larger room) and the Holy of Holies were divided by a heavy veil made of blue, purple, and scarlet fine-twined linen, richly embroidered with figures of cherubim.

Mercy Seat – In Hebrew *kaporet*, meaning "lid" or "covering," it is the lid of the Ark of the Covenant. Once a year on the Day of Atonement the high priest sprinkled blood on the Mercy Seat. It was the place where sins were covered and atonement for the high priest and the people was made. On top of the ark, at each end, stood two cherubim of gold facing each other but looking down toward the mercy seat with their wings touching each other as they were stretched out over its top.

New Covenant – A biblical term referring to a new kind of relationship between God and humanity in which sins are forgiven and each person can know God personally. This new covenant was foretold by the prophet Jeremiah (Jer. 31:31–34) and promised by Messiah Jesus at the Last Supper. It is through Messiah that this new covenant is instituted (Luke 22:20).

Shabbat Shabbaton – Literally "Sabbath of Sabbaths." Another name for the Day of Atonement (Lev. 23:32). It is therefore thought of as the holiest day in the year and a day of complete rest.

Tabernacle – Hebrew *Mishkan*. During the wilderness journey God commanded his people to construct a "tent of meeting" (tabernacle) where the sacrificial system was implemented. Moses received a blueprint directly from the Lord on how to construct a sanctuary where God's visible glory resided. The tabernacle was a prefabricated and portable structure. It had two rooms: the Holy Place and the Holy of Holies. It served for almost 500 years as the place for God to dwell among his people.

Tallit – (Tal-LEET; plural *tallitim*) Jewish prayer shawl worn over the outer clothes during the Sabbath morning service and eve of Yom Kippur.

Yom Kippur – (Yome Ki-POOR) Literally "Day of Atonement," also called Shabbat Shabbaton (Sabbath of Sabbaths) or simply the Day. Second of the Fall Feasts.

Tallitim, Jewish Prayer Shawls

The Tabernacle

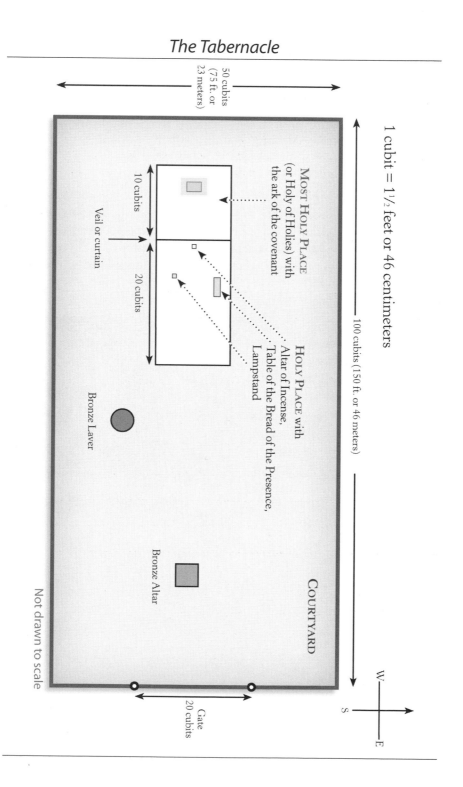

50 cubits
(75 ft. or
23 meters)

1 cubit = 1½ feet or 46 centimeters

100 cubits (150 ft. or 46 meters)

MOST HOLY PLACE
(or Holy of Holies) with
the ark of the covenant

10 cubits

Veil or curtain

20 cubits

HOLY PLACE with
Altar of Incense,
Table of the Bread of the Presence,
Lampstand

Bronze Laver

Bronze Altar

COURTYARD

W

S

E

Gate
20 cubits

Not drawn to scale

Key Bible Verses

Read: Leviticus 16:1–34 and 23:26–32

Study Question: There are many instructions given for the Day of Atonement. In your own words, what would you say was the main focus of all that was done on this holy day?

_____

_____

_____

_____

_____

Read: Hebrews 10:1–18

Study Question: What is the "once for all" sacrifice described in this passage?

_____

_____

_____

_____

_____

Read: Hebrews 10:19–25

Study Question: In what ways does the final sacrifice described in this passage change a person's relationship with God?

_____

_____

_____

_____

_____

Talk about It

Discussion Questions

1. Why do we need blood atonement as a sacrifice for our sins?

_____

_____

_____

2. Why is there no longer a need for blood sacrifices today?

_____

_____

3. Yom Kippur is called the Sabbath of Sabbaths, meaning complete rest. Why is rest so important that God commanded his people to abstain from work on the Day of Atonement?

_____

_____

_____

4. Humbling one's soul is an essential part of the Day of Atonement. How do the acceptance of atonement and the attitude of humility go hand in hand?

_____

_____

_____

5. What does it look like for people today to "humble their souls" before the Lord? What does it look like for you?

_____

_____

_____

Stop and Pray

High Holy Days Prayer

This traditional prayer is chanted through the High Holy Days season and has been passed from generation to generation for over 2,000 years. It is a prayer of hope and longing for redemption.

English
Our Father and King, be merciful to us,
For we have no deeds to commend us to you
Be merciful unto to us, According to your lovingkindness

Hebrew
Avinu Malkaynu, Chananynu Va'naynu, Ki ayn banu ma'sim Asay imanu tz'daka va-chesed, Asay imanu tz'daka va-chesed, v'hoshi-aynu

Notes:

Reflection Questions

1. Read Isaiah 53 and reflect on how Jesus is compared to a lamb led to slaughter. Then read Philippians 2:3–11 and compare how God exalted Jesus as a result of his obedience and humility. If even Jesus had to humble himself, how should this change our attitude toward others?

_____

_____

_____

_____

_____

2. Consider the price tag that sin carries. Take time to thank the Lord for his eternal provision through the once-and-for-all sacrifice, Jesus your Savior.

_____

_____

_____

_____

_____

3. Humility is essential to restoring relationship with God and each other. Think about people whom you have had problems with in the past, or people who are difficult to deal with right now. What can you do to pursue restoration in those relationships?

_____

_____

_____

_____

_____

Going Deeper

1. What was the role of the priests in Israel?

God desires to bring all people into relationship with him, but he is the one who sets the terms on how he can be approached. In ancient Israel, God could only be approached on his prescribed terms and the priests carried out this burden faithfully. The priests in Israel had the awesome responsibility of interceding on behalf of all people before the Lord.

Priesthood in Israel began with Aaron (Ex. 29:1–4), when God chose him to be the first high priest. Only Aaron's sons were able to carry the high priestly office, and other generations of Levi were common priests and Levites.

Priest did "things pertaining unto God" (Heb. 5:1). They ministered in the tabernacle and later in the temple.

- Priests watched over the altar and kept the fire going day and night.

- They made sacrifices and offerings every morning and evening on the altar.

- In the Holy Place they burned incense on the golden altar twice daily, maintaining the lampstand (Menorah) to make sure that oil would never run out, cleansing wicks to keep the light brightly burning, and keeping the table of the bread of the Presence.

- During the journeys in the wilderness the priests covered the ark and all the vessels of the sanctuary with a purple or scarlet cloth before the Levites might approach them.

- They blew "an alarm" with long silver trumpets as the people started each day on their march through the wilderness.

- Priests were educated from an early age; they would have been among the few literate persons in their society. Therefore, they were spread out among all the tribes of Israel and served as the teachers instructing all in the statutes and precepts of the Lord.

The apostle John says in the book of Revelation that Jesus "has made us to be a kingdom, priests to His God and Father" (Rev. 1:6). All believers function as "priests" unto God. Those who believe on Jesus now serve as his representatives to the world today. Believers in Jesus are now able to bring the sacrifices of praise and offerings of thanksgiving (Heb. 13:15), to keep the light of God shining brightly, and to unceasingly intercede on behalf of others through prayer. Now all who are called by his name have free access not just into the Holy of Holies, but also to the very throne of God's grace, not just once a year by one man, but any time in the moment of need.

2. How is Jesus our High Priest?

The book of Hebrews compares Jesus' ministry with that of the earthly high priests.

Earthly high priest	Messiah Jesus, the High Priest
Had to offer sacrifices for his own sins (Heb. 5:3).	Did not need to offer a sacrifice for himself because he was without sin (Heb. 4:15). Able to sympathize with our weaknesses because he became human (2:17).
Offered sacrifices for the sins of the people (5:3).	Continually intercedes for the people (7:25). Entered the inner sanctuary on our behalf (6:19–20).
All earthly priests died and thus their priesthood ended (7:23).	Made a priest forever by God (5:6, 10; 6:20). A permanent priest because he lives forever (7:24).
Offered the sacrifice of goats and bulls (9:12–13).	He is both the one who offers the sacrifice and is the sacrifice himself (7:27).
Priest by birth and ancestry (5:4).	Was not a priest by birth (7:16).
Served in the earthly copy or shadow of the real sanctuary (8:5).	Serves in the real tabernacle of heaven (8:2; 9:11, 24). Has gone through the heavens (4:14).
Served under the old covenant (7:5).	Served under a new and better covenant (8:6).
Lesser than the ministry of Messiah Jesus (7:6-7).	Ministry is greater than the priests (8:6).
His animal sacrifices were not sufficient to accomplish the removal of sin (9:9; 10:11).	His sacrifice of his own blood is able to completely remove sins (9:14; 10:14).
Offered sacrifices year after year (10:1).	Offered only one sacrifice once for all, so there is no more need for sacrifices (9:26; 10:18).
Only the high priest entered the Most Holy Place in the earthly sanctuary (9:7).	All who have faith in Jesus can confidently enter the Most Holy Place in the heavenly sanctuary (10:19).

Feast of Tabernacles

God's Finale Rally

HINT

Be sure to see the key terms and charts starting on page 85.

Follow Along and Take Notes

Session 6 Outline: *Feast of Tabernacles*

I. Feast of Tabernacles (Sukkot)

    A. Dwell in Booths

        1. Leviticus 23:42–43

    B. Gathering of the Nations

    C. Season of Our Rejoicing

    D. Feast of Ingathering

        1. Exodus 23:16

II. Symbolic Elements

    A. Lulav

        1. Leviticus 23:39

    B. Sacrifices

      1. Numbers 29:13–32

      2. 70 Bulls

   C. Water Drawing Ceremony

      1. Hallel (Psalms 113–118)

      2. Hoshiana = "save us now"

   D. Great Lights

      1. Three 75-foot candles

III. Pointing to Hope

   A. Greater Harvest

      1. Zechariah 14:16–19

      2. Deuteronomy 16:16

   B. The Kingdom

      1. Sanctuary; Ezekiel 37:26–28

2. Water will be Poured; Isaiah 44:3–4; 12:3

IV. Jesus is our Tabernacle

A. John 1:14 ("tabernacled amongst us")

B. Palm Sunday

1. John 12:12–13; Zechariah 9:9

C. Water for Thirst

1. John 7:37

D. Light

1. Isaiah 60:19–20

2. John 8:12, 20

3. Revelation 21:22

Key Terms

Great Lights – At the Feast of Tabernacles there were huge 75-foot high lampstands set up in the temple courtyard. Each lampstand had four golden oil lamps that were lit and the brilliant glow of these lights would shine throughout the city of Jerusalem. The wicks were made from the used linen garments of the priests. Throughout the seven days of rejoicing, the holy men of God would dance with torches and rejoice before the Lord around these lampstands.

Hosanna – In Hebrew *Hoshiana* ("save us now") from Psalm 118:25, one of the praise (hallel) psalms recited and sung during the Feast of Tabernacles when the crowds would wave their branches (*lulav*) before the Lord, rejoicing for seven days.

Kingdom of God – In the context of the Feast of Tabernacles, the kingdom of God is the time when according to Zechariah 14:9, "the Lord will be king over all the earth; in that day the Lord will be the only one, and His name the only one." Messiah Jesus will reign from his glorious throne and all the nations of the earth will go up to Jerusalem to worship the King, the Lord of Hosts, and celebrate the Feast of Tabernacles (Zech. 14:16–19).

Lulav – One palm branch, two willows, and three myrtle branches are bound together and waved before the Lord representing "the foliage of beautiful trees, palm branches and boughs of leafy trees and willows of the brook" (Lev. 23:40) signifying God's provision of the harvest. Today during Sukkot (Feast of Tabernacles), the lulav is waved in four directions to symbolize God's sovereignty over all the earth.

Waving the Lulav

Palm Sunday – Commemorates the evening when Messiah entered Jerusalem on a colt of a donkey and he was declared to be the King of Israel to fulfill the prophecy in Zechariah 9:9. At his triumphal entry the crowds waved their palm branches (*lulavs*) because they believed the Messiah would deliver them and establish the kingdom of God. The crowds also shouted out from Psalm 118:25, "Hosanna, Save us now," as they anticipated this deliverance.

Pilgrimage Feasts – In the Bible (Deut. 16:16–17) God commands all Israelites to appear before him or "come up to Jerusalem" three times a year: at Passover (the Feast of Unleavened Bread), Pentecost, and the Feast of Tabernacles.

Pool of Siloam – Pool of water located on the southern slope of Jerusalem where Jesus sent a blind man to be healed (John 9). It is also the pool where for seven days during Sukkot the priest would come from the temple with a golden pitcher and draw water to be poured out during the water pouring ceremony.

Shemini Atzeret – Literally "assembly of the eighth day," a sacred assembly held on the 8th day of Sukkot (Lev. 23:36).

Sukkah – Hebrew for "booth" or "tabernacle," a three-sided flimsy tent made from various branches as an observance of Sukkot. God commanded Moses in Leviticus 23:42–43 that all the native-born in Israel should dwell in booths as a memorial to the wilderness journey and God's provision and protection during the 40 years of wilderness wanderings. According to tradition, one should be able to see the stars through the roof of the booth, signifying dependence on God's protection.

Inside a Modern Day Sukkah

Sukkot – (Soo-KOTE or SOO-kote) Also called Feast of Tabernacles, Feast of Booths, and Season of Rejoicing. It represents the gathering of the nations (Lev. 23:33–43).

Temple – Hebrew *Beit ha-Mikdash*, the central place of worship in ancient Jerusalem where sacrifices were offered until its destruction in AD 70. First built by King Solomon, it replaced the wilderness tabernacle in Israel.

Transfiguration – The Greek word *metamorphoo* ("to be transformed") describes the transformation of Jesus in Matthew 17:2; Luke 9:29; Mark 9:3. A very bright light penetrated through the body of Jesus, lighting up and whitening his clothes. Jesus' disciples saw the glory that the Son of Man will have in his kingdom. At the incarnation, his glory was veiled by his human body. The Transfiguration was the out-shining of the glory of God. The veiled glory was unveiled for a few moments before these disciples.

Water Drawing and Pouring Ceremony – During the Feast of Tabernacles, the intense anticipation of rain came to be reflected in the temple services. Each morning of Tabernacles, a water libation (sacrificial pouring out of a liquid) was offered to the Lord as a visual prayer for rain for the harvest.

Wilderness Wanderings – The period when the nation of Israel was under divine discipline (Num. 13–14) for not trusting in the Lord to give them the Promised Land after they left Egypt in the Exodus. The Wilderness Wanderings lasted about 40 years, until the last person from the Exodus generation passed away (except for Caleb's and Joshua's families who had trusted the Lord).

Water and Light in the Feast of Tabernacles (Sukkot)

Ceremonies of Sukkot	The Prophesied Messiah	Jesus' Words during Sukkot	In the New Heaven, New Earth, and New Jerusalem
Seventy-five-foot high lampstands were placed in the court of the women in the temple grounds.	"I will also make You a light of the nations. So that My salvation may reach to the end of the earth." (Isa. 49:6)	"I am the Light of the world; he who follows Me will not walk in the darkness, but will have the Light of life" (John 8:12).	"And the city has no need of the sun or of the moon to shine on it, for the glory of God has illumined it, and its lamp is the Lamb. The nations will walk by its light..." (Rev. 21:23–24)
A priest carried water from the Pool of Siloam to the temple, then poured the water on the right corner of the altar.	When Messiah comes the whole earth will know God "as the waters cover the sea" (Isa. 11:9)	"If anyone is thirsty, let him come to Me and drink. He who believes in Me, as the Scripture said, 'From his innermost being will flow rivers of living water.'" (John 7:37–38)	"It is done. I am the Alpha and the Omega, the beginning and the end. I will give to the one who thirsts from the spring of the water of life without cost" (Rev. 21:6)

Get into God's Word

Key Bible Verses

Read: Leviticus 23:33–44
Study Question: What was the purpose of the Israelites living in booths (tabernacles) for seven days during this feast?

_____

_____

_____

_____

_____

_____

Read: Zechariah 14:16–21
Study Question: When the Lord reigns from his throne in Jerusalem, what feast will the nations be required to celebrate? And what will happen to the nation that does not obey the Lord?

_____

_____

_____

_____

_____

_____

Read: John 12:12–17
Study Question: When Jesus entered Jerusalem how did the crowd respond? How did Jesus' disciples respond? How did the Pharisees respond?

_____

_____

_____

_____

_____

_____

Talk about It

Discussion Questions

1. What did the sukkah (booth) in the wilderness symbolize?

    _____

    _____

2. Two themes of the Feast of Tabernacles are water and light. What do water and light represent in the Bible?

    _____

    _____

    _____

3. Why is the Feast of Tabernacles seen as the culmination of the seven feasts?

    _____

    _____

4. This study started with Sabbath, the Rest that God wants to restore to his creation. Take a few minutes to look back over the seven biblical feasts. What are some ways each of the feasts point to the restoration of God's Rest through Messiah Jesus?

    _____

    _____

    _____

5. One of the purposes of this study is to be better equipped to share the good news of Messiah with Jewish people. Now that you've finished this pilgrimage through the seven feasts, how are you better equipped to share your faith?

    _____

    _____

    _____

Prayers of Giving Thanks

There is a traditional blessing that is recited at every Jewish holiday; it applies to all the feasts as it recognizes God as our sustainer and our keeper. There is also a traditional prayer of giving thanks.

English
Blessed are You, O Lord our God, King of the universe, Who has kept us in life, and has preserved us, and has enabled us to reach this season.

Hebrew
Baruch Atah Adonai, Elohaynu Melech ha-olam, she-he-che-yah-nu v'ki-y'-mah-nu v'hi-gi-ah-nu laz'-man ha-zeh.

English
Give thanks to the LORD, for he is good, for his steadfast love endures forever.

Hebrew
Ho-du la-Adonai ki-tov, ki le-o-lam chas-do

Notes:

_____

_____

_____

_____

_____

_____

_____

_____

_____

_____

_____

_____

Think about It

Reflection Questions

1. How has the Lord provided for your protection and security over the years?

_____

_____

_____

_____

_____

_____

2. Take time to thank the Lord for the pouring out of his Spirit into your life and consider the words of Messiah and his abundant supply for you.

_____

_____

_____

_____

_____

_____

3. The Feast of Tabernacles looks forward to a time when God will make all things right in the world. What are some of the things that you most desire and hope for in the New Creation God will bring about?

_____

_____

_____

_____

_____

_____

Going Deeper

1. Why did the people wave palm branches when Jesus entered Jerusalem?

It was during Passover that Jesus entered Jerusalem on the colt of a donkey and was welcomed by multitudes of pilgrims. We read that when he was coming into Jerusalem, crowds of people came out to greet him. They took the branches of the palm trees and began to shout, "Hosanna! Blessed is He who comes in the Name of the Lord, even the King of Israel" (John 12:12–13). This was prophesied by Zechariah: "Rejoice greatly, O daughter of Zion! Shout in triumph, O daughter of Jerusalem! Behold, your King is coming to you; He is just and endowed with salvation, humble and mounted on a donkey" (Zech. 9:9). This event is traditionally called Palm Sunday.

To better understand this event, we need to understand the mind-set of first-century Jewish pilgrims. Waving palm branches on Passover is not a common Jewish custom. The only time that branches are waved is on the Feast of Tabernacles, which pictures King Messiah reigning in the kingdom with the nations from the entire world coming to worship him. During this feast a cluster of branches (lulav) made up of palm, willow, and myrtle is waved to glorify God and recognize him as ruler over the whole world (Lev. 23:40).

Though called Palm Sunday, John is the only Gospel writer who specifically mentions palm branches being waved. Matthew mentions the tender branches of the willow (Matt. 21:8) and Mark says leafy branches like the myrtle (Mark 11:8). The three accounts taken together give a picture of the lulav being waved.

If branches were to be waved at the Feast of Tabernacles to symbolize the rule of the Lord, then why were they waved when Jesus entered Jerusalem at Passover? Generally the rabbis taught: "Whatever time of year the Messiah was to appear the Jews were to greet and hail Him by taking up the Lulav clusters and singing Hosannas to Him as the Holy One of Israel" (Peskita de Rab Kahana, 27:3). Thus by waving the lulavs the Jewish people were recognizing their Messiah and King. The true King of kings, Yeshua the Messiah had arrived.

2. What kind of Messiah were the people looking for?

Though the people were waving branches hailing Jesus, the religious teachers of Israel did not accept Jesus as Messiah. Why? By the first century, Jewish religious leaders developed a system of teaching and their own interpretations of what kind of Messiah to expect.

Messianic expectations differed in the first century: Some people were hoping for a miracle worker and others were looking for a military leader. They wanted a Messiah who would fulfill their hopes and desires. Due to Roman oppression and the abuse of power, it only made sense to long for a king who would liberate them to serve God freely. Could this Jesus—who healed the sick, opened the eyes of the blind, cleansed the lepers, and preached that the kingdom of God is at hand—qualify to be the Messiah that Israel had been waiting for?

The prophets in the Bible foretold of two different roles that Messiah would fulfill:

- Messiah is pictured as ruling and reigning over the enemies of God. This is a time of peace and joy when Israel is the chief of nations again and the Lord and the Davidic throne are gloriously established in Jerusalem.

  The kings of the earth take their stand against the LORD and His Anointed [Messiah].... He who sits in the heavens laughs... "I have installed My King Upon Zion" (Ps. 2:2–4).

  Behold, days are coming' declares the LORD, "When I will raise up for David a righteous Branch, and he will reign as king" (Jer. 23:5).

- Messiah is pictured as rejected and suffering in innocence for the sins of others, even as Israel is in spiritual blindness and judgment. (See Isa. 49:7; 50:6; Ps. 22:6–16; 69:4–22; Zech. 11:12.)

  "...the Messiah will be cut off and will have nothing" (Dan. 9:26).

  "He had no beauty or majesty to attract us to Him, nothing in His appearance that we should be attracted to Him. He was a man of sorrows and familiar with suffering. Surely, He took upon

Himself our griefs and sorrows, yet we considered Him stricken by God and afflicted by Him. We did not esteem Him... Who of His generation considered Him? For He was cut off from the land of the Living for the transgressions of my people to whom the stroke was due" (Isa. 53:2–8).

Jesus fulfilled and will fulfill both Messianic expectations. He came as the suffering Messiah who laid down his life to restore humanity's relationship with God by freeing people from their sin—not only the Jewish people but all people. He is also King Messiah, but the full glory of his kingdom is yet to come. King Messiah will reign in his millennial kingdom upon his glorious throne in Jerusalem when all will be celebrating the fulfilled and ultimate Feast of Tabernacles prophesied in Zechariah 14:6.

Jewish religious leaders in Jesus' day were doubtful about Jesus' Messianic claims, and they failed to recognize him as the Messiah through his miraculous works. But even to this day, God is still reaching out to Jewish people to recognize Jesus as the Messiah who was promised throughout the Scriptures.

"Therefore repent and return, so that your sins may be wiped away, in order that times of refreshing may come from the presence of the Lord; and that He may send Jesus, the Christ [Messiah] appointed for you, whom heaven must receive until the period of restoration of all things about which God spoke by the mouth of His holy prophets from ancient time" (Acts 3:19–21).

Other DVD-Based Studies
For Individuals or Group Use

Christianity, Cults & Religions

DVD-Based Bible Study

Know what you believe and why!

Christians need to know what they believe. This excellent six-session DVD small group study teaches what the Bible says about God, Jesus, salvation, and more. It compares it to the teachings of other religions and cults. Covers Mormonism, Jehovah's Witnesses, Buddhism, Hinduism, Islam and more. Sessions led by Paul Carden, Director of The Centers for Apologetics Research and former co-host of "Bible Answer Man" radio program.

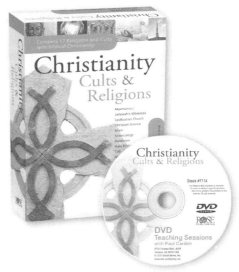

771X	Complete Kit	9781596364134
771DV	DVD	9781596364271
784X	Leaders Guide	9781596364288
785X	Participants Guide	9781596364295
404X	Christianity, Cults & Religions pamphlet	9789901981403

Four Views of the End Times

DVD-Based Bible Study

Cut through the confusion about the *Book of Revelation*

What does the Bible actually say about the end times that lead to the return of Jesus Christ? The differing ideas that divide believers into four major points-of-view are examined in this Four Views of the End Times DVD-based small group study. This new six-session study shows four different Revelation time lines and tackles Dispensational Premillennialism, Postmillennialism, Historic Premillennialism, and Amillennialism. For each view, the objective study includes simple definitions, explanation and discussion of supporting Scriptures, an overview of the view's popularity, and a focus on what we can gain from studying this perspective, and common questions and answers.

770X	Complete Kit	9781596364127
770DV	DVD	9781596364240
782X	Leader Guide: Four Views	9781596364257
783X	Participants Guide: Four Views	9781596364264
350X	Four Views of the End Times pamphlet	9781596360891

Other Products from Rose Publishing

Bible Reference Made Easy

Books, maps,
fold-out pamphlets,
Bible studies,
wall charts,
PowerPoint®
presentations

Hundreds of reproducible charts!

Full-color Bible studies

Fold-out pamphlets
These high-gloss plastic-coated
fact sheets contain hundreds of
facts and fit inside the cover of
most Bibles. They include the
most important information on
the topic at a glance.

Full-color wall charts

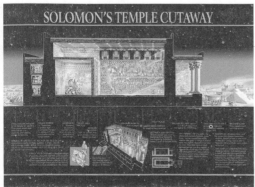

PUBLISHING

www.hendricksonrose.com

Found wherever good Christian books are sold.